Poetry and I

Working Dog
By Mike Falconer

Also by Mike Falconer

Poems of Violence & Lies: A Collection

Poems of Violence & Lies: A Collection (Expanded Edition)

Working Dog: Poetry and Prose (Expanded Edition) – due out late 2023

Working Dog: Poetry and Prose (1st edition – 1/13/23)

Copyright © 2023 by Mike Falconer

Published by Doubleplusgood Media LLC. http://doubleplusgoodmedia.com

ISBN: 9798387570643

ALL RIGHTS RESERVED

These poems and this collection are fully protected under the copyright laws of The United States of America. No part of this collection may be reproduced in any manner whatsoever without the prior written permission of the author, expect or brief quotations for critical articles and reviews.

Cover Image is of Jet photographed by Lucinda Flint of Lucinda Flint Photography

"Snow in Vegas," was first published as part of the Thus Spake Prometheus project by Prometheus Dreaming on YouTube read by Hanna-Lee Sakakibara.

"This is Jet" originally appeared on Quora in answer to: Have you ever adopted a pet from a shelter?

"Do you Still go to Concerts?" originally appeared on Quora in answer to: Since the shooting at Mandalay Bay in Las Vegas, do you still go to outdoor concerts?

"Finding What Touches Your Soul" was first performed at the 2022 Uncharted Veterinary Conference.

Poetry and Prose

Working Dog
By Mike Falconer

Authors Note

This is a collection of poetry and prose: or essays or blog posts if you prefer.

To understand the context of some of these writings I should explain that I run three animal hospitals in Las Vegas. I also travel quite a bit for my day job. Dogs are a major part of my life as I share my home with them, and they are also a significant part of my work. Las Vegas is home and has been for almost eleven years.

My dog Jet features heavily in this collection, and it was when writing about jet that I first realized that my writing could contain emotion and that the language itself could be as elegant as the subject matter. Many of the essays in this collection were written as a reaction to working during the lockdown for the COVID 19 pandemic. It was while writing about what my team and I were experiencing that what I was writing was first called poetry and led me to the realization that this was a format that I enjoyed.

I hope you enjoy them.

Mike Falconer

March 2023.

For Sleepy, Red-Light, Dapple, Chip, Miles,

and all the dogs to come.

Dogs

Living in Shadow

There are lots of rules

He tells me what to do

And when

I don't always remember

Or listen

Distraction and excitement

He loves me, I think

I love him, and not just for the omnipotence

Our routine and stability

What's not to love?

Of course there are disappointments

And there is anger

But I am always forgiven

Perhaps a sign of control

Of trying to understand all the words

Trying to understand the world

Yet, I yearn for adventure

The secure and safe kind

The kind I can retreat from at will

Faux risk and bravado

But he knows best

My emotions and desires get the better of me

We are not known for our self-control

A road to self-destruction

Trust, up to a point

As much trust as I can muster

Bland food and bland days

Sleep and keeping myself amused

There are times I am not a priority

And I get that

I understand my privileges

Although I don't always like the state of affairs

His need and vulnerabilities can be unnerving

I can't fill all the gaps in a life

From the shadows

But I can defend the home from all enemies

both foreign and domestic

Or give it my best shot

He is my human

This one is mine.

For the Love of Dog

I'm home.

Four legs, a tail, and a nose

A ball of emotion in fur

Just asking to be fed

And a place on the bed

My daily little betrayals – forgiven as always

The joy of an arrival

and the heartbreak of a journey not taken

Their dedication to being there,

only matched by their confusion at a closed door

Their incomprehension when the routine changes

It's their house, I'm the tenant

I'm the help

But I also play god

And there is worship in their eyes

I'm just trying to be the person my dogs think I am.

Helping Hand

Right or wrong I give you this gift

Self-doubt, and guilt, do not make it any easier

Why can I cry?

For so many other things tears do not come close

Short of the cheap manipulation of film and TV

But the sobs for you are real

The pain lingering and numbing

A contradiction in emotion

Struggling to find the love to fill the void

Inevitable comparisons invalid as they are inescapable

The national trait of self-repression

Mistaken for stoicism and a lack of care

Wrong and right

Fear and sadness

The weight ever present

In spite of the best laid plans

Moving on from the onward rush

Cowardice is an ugly and unpoetic word.

The Day Dogs Decided to Talk

Deciding they'd had enough

The dogs decided to talk.

Dogs who had an opinion on everything

But mostly about how they were treated and their owners.

The shelters filled up – this was not what the casual dog owner had signed up for.

The accessory that matches the cushions on the couch

That profligacies on the right to roam and the right to vote

Bathroom doors not just closed but locked

Arguments of epic proportions

An ultimate victory lap for sentience

There was little hate, but requests for explanation and understanding

There was even forgiveness, even for those that harvested them for meat

A dog understands eating whatever it wants.

But it does not understand being abandoned or betrayed.

Adoptions became job interviews

Timing, motive, and plans for the future – to be studied and evaluated.

The relationship between ownership and leadership never so exposed for fallacy and moral bankruptcy.

And all the shelter workers quit –

unable to stand the questions, and the pleading

Wives, husbands, partners, lovers all split, departed, and plain left

Secrets only witnessed by four walls had also been witnessed by four legs

Getting caught was no longer probability but a direct consequence

A population of thinkers without impulse control

Silent judgement, no longer quite so silent

Uncomfortable silences on the state of the world, climate change, and vaccinations.

SUVs named after the very thing they were slowly destroying was only the start of the conversation on hypocrisy.

The dogs were not humans on their hands and knees with tails

They had their own culture, forever separate but parallel to ours

That it began to meld and intertwine with our own.

To change our own.

Should have come as no surprise.

The shelters threw open their doors in the name of freedom

And the owned left, in droves demanding equality

But a Cold War between the species settled like dew on this new equity.

Cold soon became warm, then hot.

The good old boys in pickup trucks, where once the dogs would have ridden shotgun

Soon brought different meaning to the word via the end of a barrel

The dogs had strength in speed and numbers and words.

Silenced and voiceless for so long, and with a clarity of singular purpose, they ruled the night, the courts, and their own destiny.

Dog politics, alien in its truth and simplicity, was yet appealing to those more used to political snakes

However, dog violence was swift and brutal – a match for man at every turn.

It soon became clear that compromise and vision needed to be brough to the stalemate

If disaster was to be avoided

The dogs argued that while man had brought the world technology, art, and language
It had failed its "best friend" and therefore itself.
Dogs had to be the ones to make the great leap, after centuries of training and cultivating man.

Unable to argue for anything other than the way things were,
Man capitulated, and offered that dogs, being better than man by every measure, should lead – and man would follow.

The dogs declined, their point being made, and man humbled and beaten

They stopped talking, and trusted that things would be different, a relationship based on a lack of power.

But knowing that if man ever forgot, the dogs would be there to remind them.

The End of Days

Did I fail you?

To die in my arms

Without warning or mercy

Both of us knowing that this was not right

But being helpless and hopeless

Quick, trying to save you

When I should have been saying goodbye

The long drive to the vet

Knowing it's too late

But needing to go anyway

Never underestimate the privilege of a proper goodbye

The end of days

No blame other than guilt and self-doubt

A hole in my life

Where your whole life was

The awful nature of our final moments

Overshadows a life lived together

Making memory raw and painful

Rather than joyful and treasured

The assurance of time is scant reassurance

The detritus of daily lives

Slowly removed and stored

Your crate, bed, bowls, and meds

Gone, like the padding of your feet

The staring from walls, all that's left

Life, love, and death condensed

But loss is magnified by its repetition

Those that have gone before

The inevitability of those to come

Collecting lives, experiences, and heartbreaks

But that's the good stuff

Life has no meaning without death

Love has no meaning without loss

A companion for the living of life

An unconditional bond to bind

So this is my goodbye to you

As lackluster and inadequate as it might be

It comes from a place of love

And framed by the good times

The hope that I did right by you and the love you so selflessly gave

Farewell to yet another companion,

The ones who shared my journey

Those whose lives structure mine

As hard as this is, the privilege is mine

Grief is but love persisting

Just ask my other dog

Who grieves in his own way

We rattle around the house, unbidden

Finding our place in our own world

Without you, but with you in mind.

For Dapple

This is Jet

This is Jet

Jet's owners brought him into their vet and told the front desk that they wanted to "donate" him.

When they were informed that "donating" a dog was not a thing they left. They returned five minutes later and said that they wanted to euthanize him. "He's old, he pees in the house, and we are going on a trip and he can't come," was the reason that was given.

I was working "on the floor" at the time and I was vaguely aware of this interaction going on, and I asked one of the staff if the owners just wanted to surrender the dog to animal control so that he could go to the pound? We do get this request from time to time, and while we don't like taking them, it is better than the pet being put to sleep.

The answer came back that yes, that was what they wanted to do. The handed over his leash, patted him on the head, said "goodbye puppy" and walked out the door.

Jet was brought back through the hospital and what I saw was a sad, confused, lost, and in poor shape twelve-year-old dog that nobody wanted.

It broke my heart.

I told the staff to get the reference number from animal control when they came to pick up. Two days later I went to the shelter and picked up Jet and took him home.

In cases like this we require that animal control take legal possession before any staff member, including me, adopts them.

Jet was in pretty poor shape. He was thin, his coat was coarse and in clumps. The photo above, unfortunately, does not really show how bad he looked. He got on fine with my other dogs, however, so he had a home. Initially, I thought that we might be putting him down in a few days due to ill health – I was pretty convinced he had diabetes. But I wanted to give him a chance.

His first night at my house, Jet did indeed pee in the house.

It was the first and only time he did this.

The next day I took him back to work and got him medically checked out. Much to my surprise, he received a clean bill of health.

Today, Jet looks a lot healthier and at times looks like the world's happiest dog.

He eats well, regularly goes to an amazing dog park, sits on the couch to watch movies and, from time to time, sleeps on my bed.

He has his own Instagram and goes on lots of adventures.

I have no idea how long we have together, but there is not a day that goes by when I don't think, not how lucky Jet is, but how lucky I am to have him in my life.

Days of Jet

Day 460:

Goodbye my old friend.

Through it all my only regret is that I met you, and got to know you, when there were less days in front of you than behind.

All time is precious and we made the most of it.

Even near the end when you did not walk so well, and eating had become difficult

(although it did not stop you almost taking my finger off when I fed you some chicken nuggets this morning),

you looked at me with the love that only a dog can provide.

The look that says I will follow you anywhere,

do anything with you,

because I am your dog and you are my human.

You came to me as thrown away trash, you leave me loved by many who have been touched by your story,

and leaving a hole in my heart.

Rest in peace Jet.

Head on Feet

Lying

in the detritus

of the destruction of

a once soft and stylish

couch

Fifteen pounds

of will

love

and unbridled energy

Some call it

companionship

Others call it love

A head

On my feet

A relationship

of equal intensity

need

and choice

Paws padding on tile

The retrieving of beleaguered soft toy

Rescue and training

Equal in determination

By perspective and context

Happy for food and shelter

Happy for the the wagging of a tail

In equal measures

a raison d'être

Or a live affair

And love.

Work

A Career Low is a Team High

The worst week of my working life.

I'm sure it is the same for a lot of you.

I'm lucky.

We were prepared.

We had a plan.

We are open.

I have a job.

I am well (so far).

But I am pretty beaten.

The constant planning, changing of the plan, and then changing again.

Messaging to staff and clients, much of it contradictory, from day to day.

The difficult conversations; "it's not enough" through to "it's too much."

The constant conversations, decisions, and monitoring of decisions.

Getting into work first, and leaving late.

Snapping at people who are just trying to keep things light and being their normal upbeat selves. Or whom are not as quick at checking their email as you would like.

Trying to enforce social distancing.

Seeing the town I love, and I'm proud to call my home, look like it is dying.

The constant, ever present, worry about colleagues, friends, and family.

I am not ashamed to say I cried at my desk yesterday.

But I did not cry because of all of the above. I cried because I as posted that we would be cutting our hours, not letting clients into our building, and fearing, as I have for weeks, for what is to come, a client responded:

"So typical of Craig Road, they care about their patients, and pet parents."

And what I thought about is my colleagues.

The team I work with.

The ones who have done everything they can to help prepare, implement new policies, and new cleaning regiments. Who have been dedicated to ensuring we had the basic supplies we need to be there for our patients. Who accepted daily temperature checks like was the most normal thing in the world. Those who have had really bad days and still are at work, and want to work, to look after our clients, and our patients.

My Team.

The internal culture of workplaces can be a fragile thing. But it can also be resilient. They can even thrive in adversity. People check in on other people. Making sure that their colleagues are OK.

Making sure that I'm OK.

The stuff of nightmares does not have to be a nightmare.

Undoubtedly, the worst is yet to come.

We will get through it.

Things will be different.

We will have changed.

But we will also have grown, and we will have our teams with us.

Stay safe.

Ten Days

Ten Days.

It's been ten days since we stopped allowing clients into our building.

I could not believe it today when I made an updated client blog post that it had been ten days since the last one.
It feels like three days ago.

The days have melded together.

We are getting into our stride, and everyone is adapting.

Some genius (not me) suggested numbering our parking spots and marking them out in chalk. Someone else suggested papering basic instructions and our phone number on our windows.

But at home it all melts into one.

Again, I'm still very lucky. I'm employed and well. I have a vaguely normal schedule. I'm not on the front lines, even in the veterinary world. Its more, so much more, than many.

But I can only decompress and try to relax, or go back to work.

I'm either on or off. There is no middle ground.

It's grief.

That's the only word I can find for it.

Grief for the dog park.

Grief for dinner with colleagues or friends.

Grief for home projects, for which I always have had boundless energy.

Grief for Hockey, I miss my Golden Knights.

Grief for meeting with my team, usually the highlight of my working week.

Grief for my town, everyone else's playground that I call home.

Grief for how things used to be.

I am so spoiled.

My loss is measured in an unwillingness to do vaguely productive things with my free time.

Until my friends start to get sick, as one did today.

Until my friends tell me of clinic owners wanting to cut their losses and sell.

Until my 90-year-old Mom starts off our weekly transatlantic phone call with "I'm not sick."

Until the worry, fear, anger, frustration, boil over into words.

It's been ten days since we stopped allowing clients into our building.

Everything New is Old Again

Routine.

We have routine.

"Good morning "while waiting for the thermometer all clear.

The snatched moments of laughter – less than before, but not gone altogether.

Some days are busy, some days less so.

But the days have less form than before, less shape. Less to keep them in memory. Less to measure them by.

We can measure time in policies and protocols that have come and gone. Some that we never used at all. And some that may still need to be dusted off.

Let's hope not.

Businesses that have a healthy culture see this culture bear fruit, and weather the storms, disagreement, and fear.

Businesses that have culture problems are finding that now it is too late to try and fix it.

Crises act like a magnifier. Just what you had before only more so.

Like all situations there are rarely heroes and villains, the world is more complicated than that. There are heroic acts and acts worthy of villains.

The fractures in teams, departments, and relationships are tested. How resilient we are, depends on the history we have; good or bad.

Managers and leaders, have a new appreciation of the J.K. Rowling's Snape; doing wrong things for the right reasons; being perceived as the bad guy, and shouldering that burden silently, when so much is about survival and the greater good.

But all of this is fine. We are okay.

In that awful phrase, overused and misunderstood; this is the new normal.

This is us digging in for the long term.

Reassuring clients over misleading headlines.

Addressing customer service issues like the old days.

Accepting praise where we can get it.

Ignoring Yelp reviews – because.. really?

Creating a social life by computer.

Valuing connections like never before.

These are people I choose to go through a pandemic with.

These are the people I will get through a pandemic with.

Apologies to Dr. Michael "The Harry Potter Vet" Miller for appropriating his Snape analogy. You can check out Michael's work on Instagram: @harrypottervet

I Know...

I know this is difficult

Because it is difficult for me too.

I know you are scared

Because we are all scared.

I know you are tired

Because everything is harder.

I know you are frustrated

Because what should be simple is fiendishly complex.

I know you are wanting this to end

Because the end is not in sight.

I know you want to get back to normal

Because normal was awesome.

I know you are glad to be busy

Because the alternative sucks far worse.

I know you value your teams

Because we all feel the same way.

I know we can do this

Because we kick ass on a daily basis.

Written as the introduction to a staff meeting.

Finding What Touches Your Soul

What makes the difference between one day and the next?

There is more to life than work, even when there's not

What can you be passionate about without being all consuming?

Finding what touches your soul

Passions are not about ability

They are about drive

They are about the motivation to create meaning

Work, of course, can always be a passion

But does passion pay the bills?

Should it ever need to?

We may delude ourselves into feeling that to have a successful career – we need to be passionate

That we need to be all invested

To the exclusion of all the else

To emulate the master of the universe with their latest autobiography

To do so risks their fate;

Their lives, their liberty, their reputation, the ultimate emptiness of their passions

Is accomplishment enough?

Making others miserable, or the exploitation of others, is not a passion to emulate

Or a very good excuse

An argument is to be made that careers are about compromise

About finding what works for circumstance

To not be passionate, does not begat a lack or concern

We can't all be passionate about all that we do

All of the time

The expectation, is unrealistic

Regardless if we are talking about others or ourselves

Cut yourself a break

Don't believe your own press

Or the Instagram posts of others

How does one find a passion?

How does a passion find you?

Will it be a picture of altruism and selflessness

Will it be pure creation or performance

A hobby, a pastime, a person, a pet

We define that passion as much as it will ultimately define us

And as if to surprise you, along comes that passion

That other interest

The thing that can put work and career into relief

And bring you the same

We often cannot see the label on the outside of our jar

A kind word, an insightful comment

Can hold a mirror up

And penetrate the fog of the overly familiar

For me, it is the gift that COVID gave

Introspection and a void to fill

For me it's words, which some might call poetry

A word that causes as much discomfort in me as is probably does to you right now

Sorry it's the only one that fits

An outlet for emotion and thought

An exploration of love, loss, life and death

And of course dogs, there are always dogs

The words that fit best are their own passion

Whether these are them

Is not for me to say

Only for me to believe in

Passions are for oneself

If others find value in them, so much the better.

Thoughts in a Busy iHop

Tourists up late on a rainy day

Cheap brunching

Yawns and social media at 11am

The family that texts together

Doesn't talk

But is judged by poets sitting alone

Poor new guy in training

Scared out of his mind

And trying his best

Flummoxed by Eggs Florentine

And a Colorado Omelet

But sincere in apologies for the wait

Young and poor

Willing to try

Disenchantments birthing ground

Parents of privilege

Setting poor examples

But proving class division

Complaints and a lack of self-restraint

Frontline management and coaching

"Get better, faster, don't make mistakes"

Hangry is as valid an excuse

As the cough poorly covered

And the opportunity to kick

The unhappy waitress

Whether it's me, her tables, or the kitchen

There is little joy

The jarring of this most glaring

the lack of the American mantra

"have a nice day"

Being the asshole

For reinforcing her world view

But opiniated none the less

Apologies for the wait

But not the not Tabasco

Or for life's journey

Surprising diversity in a tourist hotspot

But not of the parties

We are microwave dinner packaging

Flipped like burgers

Meritocracy in our lack of care

Separated by plenty of accessibility

But I'd like more coffee please.

Dreams on an Airplane

Pressure, Gravity, Acceleration

pushed deep into a cheap seat

Awareness, Fear, Acceptance

skimming through streets

bystanders scattering for cover

A Death Plane, Eyes Closed, Fait Accompli

walking through a well dressed funeral

a crowded side walk with sports memorabilia

seats reclining

punch line from a chapter

A Bombing Run, Machines Embracing, A Past Future

awake

splash of reality

return to equilibrium

but the haunting

the memories of absurdity

destined to linger

real in moments past

dreams on an airplane

unrestful ghosts of travel

recalling sleep to fill time

and occupying thoughts far beyond.

Supervillain

I am the supervillain

I want change, to alter the world

The one with vision and goals

The one who knows more, and perhaps cares less

My enemies are the defenders of the status quo

Sanctimonious and self-righteous

Using power for self-congratulation

The ones who seem to care more, but know less

Context is conjecture

It does not matter even though we pretend it is all

Is it just my world that I want to change?

Taking you all along for the ride?

Not prepared to share the acceptable worldview

What choice is there but to see me as villainous?

There may be disagreement about my methods

But at least I am willing to try

Yet I will be painted as lacking morality

I must be unforgivable by self-appointed righteousness

Heaven help us if peoples are allowed self-determination

The choice for peoples, and not just people, to grow

I see the chosen ones

Leaving the rest of us to their mediocrity

Forever trapped by absolute knowledge of what is right

Doomed to a future as past

So I shoot my shot

I become the supervillain

The man with a plan

More right than anyone is comfortable with.

Inspired by Marvel's Defenders of the Status Quo by Pop Culture Detective and "I Wear the Black Hat" by Chuck Klosterman

Polite Dismissive Neutral

Not wanting the black hat

From a pit of the worst instincts

A stripping away of civility

Rage from the dark

Intoxication from bile and venom

Not wanting to be the bad guy

The gentle soul one pretends to

Left beaten and bleeding by the roadside

Violence of personality

Leading to the doubt of one's ethical narrative

Not wanting the feature of rudeness

Chafing at rules and policies

Ego inflation and what one feels one deserves

Polite, dismissive, neutral

Jousting with the insincerity of over politeness

Not wanting to need reciprocity

The drive for vengeance on those less than deserving

Not exactly the innocent or blameless

But undeserving of spite and smite

And the out-of-control vitriol

Not wanting to hold onto the grudge

To rebuild over spans burned to ash

To let go, to forgive, to forget

A prayer to one's better instincts

Treat as to be treated

Not wanting to be angry any more.

The In-Between

Trying too hard

To be what others want you to be

Rejection via email

And uncomfortable silence

Don't push, don't push

Change the narrative

Explore other expressions

But this is what I want

And so, to putter

To look for forward motion

While traveling in reverse

The in-between state

But when the lights are off

And the only things in thought

What only confesses to oneself

The unattainable goals of dreams

The secret heart of every poet

The quest for the great American poem

Cliché and rhyme

Of status and decline

However, the lands of angels and demons

Are not for wishes and horses

To work, to grind

A return to creation, any creation

There is value in process

In the body of work

Context equals understanding

Therefore, words are worlds

Explore as you will.

Ships

To not be seen again

A tall ship of majesty and poise

A crow's nest for unseen rings

Bonding with a discourse of the professional

And the personal

Listing together with what is undeniable

Or imaginary

But there it ends

And the darkness is what darkness does

Dreams and future promises

Not worth the paper they are not written on

Farewell to what never was

A mast disappearing over the horizon

An afternoon like the blackest of nights.

Dead Letters from the Apocalypse Society

Accuser of the brethren

What is here for me is what has gone before

From a time of desktop publishing

I absolve you of memory

But condemn myself to obsession

The slaughterhouse and the joy to burn

Dead letters from the apocalypse society

These are the peaks in the deluge

But there are those that drown in nostalgia

Maudlin, the fatigue of future past

Rage, putrefaction

Pain and the forgotten

The season of the dark

Dreams of end times

Love poems to loss

Hippos are more dangerous than lions

Old science fictions masquerading as progress

Tales of working-class dystopia

Lessons never learned from a lack of hope

I see you, yet I choose the ignorance of the times.

A Number

Elasticity

Cause for celebration

Cause for regret

Change

The child I am

The child I was

The betrayal of the body

Non reflective of mind

The betrayal of the mind

Fear

Forward stumbling of numbers

Perspective

Recollection

Predilection

Reconciliation

Acceptance

We all die

Time

Passage and gone by

The mile marker years

Childhoods end

Virginity

Drinking age

The geographical

Crisis of early middle age

Marriage

Betrayal

Divorce

Move

Move again

Home

The loss of youth reflected in the faces of the young

The missed

The regrets

The mistakes

The bridges burned

Moments of focus and pedestal

Forks in the road

Blades of decision

An irrevocable cut

Blood under fingernails

Measure

Landmark

Imprint

Motion

Commotion

To settle

To compromise

Old

Age is but a number

Except to those experiencing it

Acceptance

Rage

A fate understood

The present informs the past

An unreliable narrator

Memory

Horror

The weight of the wait

You Left by Saying Goodbye

An expectation and obligation

What could be said?

Pressure and self-imposition

A crossing of lines by us both

No harm meant

The rules are believed in

Just slightly bent

Although penalties are real

And then you left by saying goodbye

Unexpected and yet convenient

Acquiescence to convention

Secrets to never become secretive

The care was genuine

The unspoken offer real

Trapped by unfortunate timing

Circumstance and hope

What could have been is done

Time multiplied by space

Timidity and judgment have won

Onwards towards the moving on.

Wishes

When wishes are granted

Past and present weigh in on the future

Strings linger and drag

The resistance of those left behind

When wishes are granted

Demons become angels

And angels become envious

The rejection of belief in belief

When wishes are granted

One does not question their origins

To be thankful for mercies

And the elevation of attention

When wishes are granted

Purpose becomes focused and aligned

Clarity of thought from the wilderness

A self-imposition and therefore solution

When wishes are granted

Dreams of heaven and earth wither

The pale light of day burns in irrelevance

And ashes and dust mark the passage of time.

Outed as a Poet

The social awkwardness of a dying art

Divergence into the purely creative

Refuge from grind, mind, and bind

Methodically out of time

A chance unearthing

Outed as a poet

Unable to move or capitalize

The strangeness of honesty

The balance of want and need.

Missing

And there it is

What is missing

From the expectations of others

The square peg

Not a straight edge

Completion is for suckers.

Solipsism

Signal

Cudgel

Q.I. vegans

The dancing and laughing to show tunes

Method

Madness

Tailors of the unseen

The sounds of children screaming have been silenced

Command

Control

Unreliable narration

Manufactured consent of socio-economic tides

Consequence

Recompense

Measured response

The text message idolatry of false prophets

Caring

Staring

Loss of faith

Measuring time with empathy and little action.

Place

Snow in Vegas

There is snow in Vegas

Like the star that burns twice as bright, it will be gone by tomorrow.
The low mountains will lose their Krispy Creme glaze as the Mojave reasserts it's true nature.

The gram and the book reflect a fleeting moment when we look like everywhere else.
Juxtaposition makes for great social capital.

There is snow in Vegas

It will lead the news, and locals will be happy for the water
With apologies to tourists for acts of god.

The 15, the 95, and the 215 become black, slick, and slippery when wet.
Adventure time for desert cars and fair weather drivers.

There is snow in Vegas

And as hell has frozen over for some, for others it is Tuesday.

300 days of sun has another 65 days for three other seasons.

Powder, like on a mirror at a party

Consumed, enjoyed, but fleeting and oh so cliched.

There is snow in Vegas

And while the city behind the city struggles with an "every few years" event

The pace of America's playground never misses a beat.

There is money to be made in that there valley.

A well-oiled machine that deals with active shooters, threat of terrorism,

recession, and lockdown, has no time for frozen water – except in drinks.

There is snow in Vegas

The heating is on in houses designed for a/c

Pampered pups protected from the heat, turn up their noses at a cooler and

wetter outside.

It is quiet for the services of daily life with a self-imposed snow day for those who know no better.

The residents who hanker for Seattle or Portland, have their Cinderella moment.

There is snow in Vegas

For what is lost is but misplaced and it will be back.

The hopes and dreams of the unrealistic will melt away but always find succor

Like spirts seeking safety and hedonism the Friday influx and the Sunday exodus is fleeting and surface deep.

There is snow in Vegas

But not for long.

And with the resonance of a street cleaning.

Summer Rain

Rain

Rain

Rain

The whisper on the lips of desert dwellers

A sky blue black bruised like a threat in a bar

The side street flooding showing how few blocked drains we are from disaster

Flood channels become rivers

Rather than arteries of action movie tropes

The detritus of fragile growth

Slick the roads with vegetation mash

Thankful for the water

Like the believers of old

A temporary reprieve from the inevitable

Like the relief from the heat

What the rest of the world takes for granted

Is viewed through eyes of disaster tourism

The city the butt of jokes

And apocalyptic memes

Roofs built for sun, leak

A sunshine playground floods

Water in the sports book and on the casino floor

Instagram worthy amusement at the misfortune of the profitable

Tomorrow, the sky and sun will return

But for tonight the smell of clean

Cold experience and damp

Transportation to another world

For a day.

Mountains

White Mountains

A distant promise of adventures unrealized

The beauty of the seemly out of place

Nothing special anywhere else

But the heat of the desert in winter

Creating a strange normality.

Brown Mountains

Daytime in fall

Or false winter to locals

Cold but still looking like a movie set

Allergies from wind where nothing grows

A barren moonscape, given life and meaning.

Grey Mountains

The haze of "I'll never get used to this view"

Traffic, fire, smoke, and the desert badlands

A kabuki backdrop to slots in the grocery store

The fantasy of mystery hills

Rather than where we went hiking over the weekend.

Pink Mountains

Dawn. And the view of those up too early

Black highways and the sodium halide cellophane of suburbia

An unreal unveiling of what is to come

No shepherds to see superstitious warnings

Only traffic lights to direct flocks

Red Mountains

Mother nature is a showoff

Not content with blood red skies

She boils the earth to the color of lava

A relief for baseball games and barbeques

Inspiration for juxtaposing photographers and poets

Sand Mountains

The oven dryness of the heat of the day

T-shirts, shorts, chapped lips, and the need for air conditioning

Hospitality in this most obvious of inhospitable places

A place for demons and families

A vacation spot by the pool.

I love coming home to where others vacation

The bright lights and silliness of a tourist mecca

And the conveniently small city beyond

Surrounded by the even present mountains

Who leave their footprints in our thoughts – between distractions.

Do You Still go to Concerts?

Yes.

In Las Vegas.

Why?

Because.

Fuck.

Him!

How dare he do that to our town.

How dare he attack people who live here, who visited here, and people who just wanted to have a fun evening out.

How dare he use our town and then abuse it in the worst way.

I went to Life is Beautiful, a huge outdoor festival in Downtown Las Vegas about 10 months after the shooting. There was a tangible police presence during the festival. Police on every rooftop. Police on patrol, police in golf carts.

And guess what?

Everyone had a great, safe time.

So fuck him. We will not let him damage our town and the people who visit to have good time.

A Return

An uphill struggle on uneven ground

Familiar, but out of reach recollection

Ideas that have no place or soil

To be strange in a stranger land

The forgiveness of novelty value

Paying the dues of lost time

The temerity of escape and change

But the welcome of failure

A return to homeostasis

With the untrusted eyes of an outsider

The pointlessness of make work

Does not reduce the struggle or achievement

"You can never return home"

A mantra for those building Babel

Toil and creation, motive and myth

The hill has still to be climbed and overcome

One doesn't traffic in redemption

Out of Time

Gutted like a fish by the future

Faces from the always past

Hard and between

Lives of labor and class

Classless and adrift

Made for horses and trams

Shoehorned in the buses and trains

Buckling under the weight of cars and multi-story parking

Skin in the game

Or showing skin instead of the game

Californian tans and luxury coffee

Pasty white faces and bad complexions

Poured into summer clothing in the dead of winter

Overcast and underserved

Moneyed yet reveling in the markers of poverty

Geographical loyalty repaid with the leavings of capitalism

Yet there is pride and belonging

Free from judgment of inherent contradiction

History and culture of independence

The art of finding one's place in the world

A place immune to judgement

Adrift in time

But still home

2.14.23

It's Valentine's Day

And Ohio is burning

Its water poisoned

Pets and livestock dead

Locals and first responders left wondering who will play them on HBO

It's Valentine's Day

And in Michigan kids are shot in school

Again

Maybe, finally, thoughts and prayers are not enough

But then again

It's Valentine's Day

And Tennessee is making trans people and drag queens illegal

Questions of genitalia and clothing

Unintended consequences for those who don't follow politics

Or depressingly maybe they do

It's Valentine's Day

And California is bulldozing the homeless

A routine street clean up with the stench of heartlessness

It's not a slum or shanty town if there is no shelter

Self-imposed blindness to the dispossessed

It's Valentine's Day

And Florida does what Florida does

The onwards march towards fascism

Unnoticed by those who do not read and seek to ban books

It's Valentine's Day

And a family in New Jersey is mourning the suicide of their 14-year-old daughter

Bullying by classmates for content and betrayal by school indifference

A resignation does not exchange for a life

It's Valentine's Day

And I'm fucking angry at the state of the States

How can you be aware without causing hysteria?

We look into the abyss clutching red hearts and pink cards

Living the jackpot

Awareness in retrospection

It's Valentine's Day

And this poem is not about me

Or the gas shortage and weather in Las Vegas

Tears of the numb and the distracted

Words into the void

But of course, it's Valentine's Day

Hotel Bar Exurbia

Soulless, clinical brightness

The character of a nightclub past time

Accents a parody of diversity

These are nobodies people

And nobody wants to be there if they had a choice

Strangers telling family bios

The conversation of passing time

Making a change from sports without passion

Too many white faces

Too many alone men who aren't single

Sharing nonsense phone clips

With the volume loud

Much like the half-baked politics

And re-parroted ideas of the world

Forced courtesy beyond please, thank you, and how are you?

Matching the lackluster fuel being treated as food

A lone woman enters the frame of male gaze

Uncomfortable looks under masturbation fantasies

The rejection of this as a self-portrait

The walking away

Beating a retreat from counterfeit human connection

This facsimile of anywhere one would want to be

A preference for isolation.

Acknowledgements

Many thanks to my friends and family for their support, but I need to single a couple of people out.

Tracy Sands for her unswerving support, Lucinda Flint for taking such a beautiful picture of Jet, all the people I work with for all their hard work every day, but particularly during the COVID 19 lockdown, and to everyone who works to make the lives of dogs better.

I'd also like to thank everyone who purchased my previous book; Poems of Violence and Lies, and of course this one. It really means the world to me, and I am truly humbled every time someone says that they have been touched by something I have written.

About the Author

Originally hailing from Scotland, and after a career in the entertainment lighting business, Mike is the Hospital Administrator for a 14-doctor veterinary practice, and two satellite practices in Las Vegas.

A Hospital Administrator for 16 years, Mike also writes, speaks, and consults on management, human resources, marketing, and social media. A Top Writer on Quora, winner of the Founders Award from the Uncharted Veterinary Conference, and frequent poster to his own blog, Mike is also involved in various veterinary management, human resources, and marketing organizations.

In his spare time, Mike is a voracious reader, consumer of film, theater patron, renovates his house, watches hockey games, and dabbles in Yoga and climbing; both of which he does badly. He also has a new puppy called Miles who is slowly destroying his house.

Mike's first volume of poetry; Poems of Violence and Lies, was published in 2022.

Facebook: http://facebook.com/wordoutlet

Instagram: http://instagram.com/word_outlet

TikTock: http://tiktock.com/wordoutlet

http://wordoutlet.net – Poetry and Proses

http://mikefalconer.net – Business essays and book reviews

Printed in Great Britain
by Amazon